You look great, but how do you sound?

Dr. June Johnson

Published by: Management Strategies, Inc.

Published by:
MANAGEMENT STRATEGIES, Inc.
PO Box 191 ● Cedarburg, WI 53012

Contact:
June Johnson, DMA
Voice Power
500 W. Bender Road, Suite 67
Milwaukee, WI 53217
phone: 414/332-0926 ● fax: 414/332-6462
email: VoicePwr1@aol.com
http://www.wisonline.com/VoicePower

FIRST EDITION

ISBN# 1-888475-07-2

Library of Congress Catalog Card # 98-091467

Cover Design: Jim Taugher, CI Design

Printed in the United States of America

This book is dedicated to:

My daughter Anne Elizabeth Koepsell and my son Jay Norman Johnson, the most important people in my life. They put up with their mother through all of her performances and practice sessions and have fully support me in this, my current career.

I also thank them for my grandchildren, Bianca Anne Koepsell, Eric Hans Koepsell and Tyler Jay Johnson, who have added a third dimension to my life.

Acknowledgements

To Judy Bridges, without whom this book would not have been written. She supported, encouraged and bolstered me as she pushed, prodded and goaded until the book was finally completed. Without her suggestions and revisions this book would not be in your hands today. Not only has Judy served as a mentor, she has become a very special and dear friend.

To Barry Eigen, my mentor and friend, whose help in planning and shaping my business has been invaluable,and to whom I owe so much.

To Jack Pachuta, who handled the final details of printing and publishing while providing important technical guidance that kept me from floundering and losing precious time.

Contents

INTRODUCTION

I have been lucky enough to spend my entire professional life doing what I love most - singing and performing. I began singing before I can remember and never once doubted that was what I wanted to do with my life. As professor of voice at Eastern Illinois University, I enjoyed the best of both worlds - the opportunity to perform regularly in opera, concert, recital and music theater, and the chance to teach promising young singers, many of whom have gone on to successful careers in opera and music theater.

After taking early retirement and moving to Milwaukee, Wisconsin, I turned to using my knowledge of voice and performance to helping people speak effectively. This book is the result of over eight years of coaching and facilitating voice workshops.

We're not born to speak effectively. Articulation is not particularly important to toddlers. They struggle to express themselves, often with comical results. When my youngest grandson, Tyler, was a toddler, his efforts to speak were so earnest and garbled my son referred to them as Tylerbonics.

In learning to speak, children are influenced by the voices and speech habits of those around them. Parents and grandparents take great pride in teaching them to increase their vocabulary. But in school the emphasis is on reading and writing, despite the fact that throughout our lives we spend far more time speaking than reading or writing. Still, example is the best teacher. Candice Bergen speaks with beautiful articulation, due in no small part to the fact that her father, ventriloquist Edgar Bergen, had to articulate his words clearly if his dummies, Charlie McCarthy and Mortimer Snerd, were to be understood.

Through my programs, I encounter many individuals who are unhappy with the sound of their voice and believe there is nothing they can do about it. If you are unhappy with yours, don't go through life believing you can't change it. The voice is a very flexible instrument. Never underestimate its power.

As you work through this book, you will receive the necessary tools that will help you improve your voice and communication skills. Just as you spend time on improving your physical image, time spent on improving your vocal image will prove very rewarding.

The knowledge that you speak well will do wonders for your image and self-confidence. And if Helen Keller and Marlee Maitlin, both deaf since early childhood, could learn to speak, you should have no problem improving your speech.

Chapter One

YOU LOOK GREAT
But how do you sound?

As a man speaks, so is he.

Publius Syrus

Y ou dress for success, diet to stay trim, exercise to stay slim and eat to stay healthy. But how do you sound?

In business and social situations the impression you make is determined largely by how you sound. Your voice leaves a far more lasting impression than your appearance.

According to recognized experts, billions of dollars are lost each year in missed opportunities and squandered sales all because of the ineffective way people speak.

The Internet, e-mail, voice mail, faxes and modems have all had their impact on communication. Technology that was beyond our comprehension just a few years ago now enables us to communicate easily and quickly anywhere in the world. But despite all of these incredible advances, nothing will ever take the place of the human voice. The spoken word has always been and always will be the most important means of interpersonal communication.

Whether you're speaking one on one, giving a presentation before a group, chairing a committee or selling on the telephone, how you use your voice is critical.

First impressions

When I started voice coaching a number of years ago, my first client was a young man recommended to me by a speech therapist. Mike was a tall, good-looking architect who wanted to apply for an opening at a more prestigious firm. My first impression on meeting him was that he did not need voice therapy, he needed vocal coaching. He lacked self-confidence. He would need to address that problem head-on before interviewing for any position.

We worked together every week for over two months to bring the depth to his voice that would convey authority. He had it within him, he only needed to believe he did. When Mike felt his confidence growing, he arranged for the interview. When he came back to tell me about it, he was full of smiles. "I spoke with such confidence," he said, "that I didn't know myself." My day was made and voice power was born.

Improving his speech had done wonders for Mike's image and self-confidence. As a postscript to this story, I'm happy to report that Mike went into a more prestigious architectural firm.

You can accomplish the same with your voice and realize the same success Mike did. Little else helps your self-confidence and ego more than knowing you speak well.

Public examples

It's no accident that Ronald Reagan was called the "Great Communicator." As an actor, he was trained to speak well and use his voice to move, persuade and inspire. When he was in public office, he was able to use this skill to put his message across.

Bob Dole, on the other hand, may have lost his bid for the presidency because of the way he spoke. He was boring to listen to. His voice lacked vitality and energy, giving the impression that he wasn't particularly interested in what he was saying.

To speak well, you first need to have an interest in what you are saying, and then say it with interest. How you hear yourself is not necessarily how others hear you.

How much thought and attention have you given to your voice? How you speak permeates everything you do and reveals so many things about you-your educational level, professional competence, personality, mood, attitude toward others and feelings about yourself.

While I was in school in New York City, studying voice at Juilliard, I had a monthly lunch date with four fellow students. One particularly lovely spring day, we decided to make our lunch a very special occasion by dining at a fancy restaurant, one that actually used table cloths.

The restaurant we chose was not very large, but it was impressively located in the converted basement of an old brownstone mansion on Manhattan's lower east side. And it was noted for the number of celebrities who dined there.

We arrived early and dallied through lunch, keeping our eyes on the door in hopes that we would see someone famous. As we were finishing our meal, the door opened with a flourish that caught every one's attention.

Standing in the doorway was one of the most beautiful women I have ever seen. She was the epitome of elegance. She was tall, blonde and beautifully dressed, a photographer's dream. All conversation ceased as every eye focused on her.

The woman paused, or should I say "posed," in the doorway. When she was sure she had everyone's attention, she glided across the room to the bar. There, she leaned on her elbow and, with a nasal twang for all to hear, said to the hostess, "Mabel, wudja tell Goitrude I can't meeder? I gotta go tuh acyapuncture at two."

The women, so beautiful to look at, totally destroyed the wonderful impression she had first made and was completely unaware of it.

Think of your voice as your "vocal writing."

You can get by with poor handwriting, but not with poor "vocal-writing."

Illegible handwriting may or may not affect how you are perceived. But unintelligible speech, poor articulation or lazy speech is a serious problem.

First impressions are made in the first ten to fifteen seconds and are often difficult to change. Physical characteristics tend to fade into the background, vocal characteristics do not.

Learn to make the most of your voice. With the lessons and exercises in this book, you can develop the sound you and others like to hear.

Summary:

Be aware of what your voice says about you.

Make your voice work for you, not against you.

Develop a vocal image that complements your physical image.

Chapter Two

WHERE TO BEGIN

Mind your speech a little,
lest you should mar your fortunes.

William Shakespeare

A s with anything that is worth achieving, speaking effectively takes work and determination. There are no short cuts. To change habits of long standing requires time and practice, but if the determination is there results will follow. Set a goal for yourself that is realistic, outline your plan and follow it.

There is no magic formula

Practice is the key word. If you have ever learned to play an instrument or to shoot baskets, you know how important practice is. The same principle holds true for the voice. Invest your time and effort, and success will follow.

I have had clients who applied themselves with regular and thoughtful practice and improved their speech immeasurably in a short space of time. It usually takes at least six weeks of steady practice to change habits and achieve goals.

Remember, your goal is to be heard and understood.

Use a tape recorder

If you don't already own a tape recorder, invest in one. It need not be expensive and will prove one of the best investments you can make. Use it with the exercises. It will help you to understand your voice and identify the habits that need to be changed.

Listen to your voice

To know your voice you must learn to listen to it with a critical ear. When you understand how it sounds you will be better equipped to evaluate what you need to do to improve. Keep your tape recorder handy and use it.

I also recommend listening to other speakers. As a singer, I always learned a great deal about both what to do and what not to do from listening to other singers. Identify what you like and don't like and what makes one speaker interesting and another difficult to listen to. Then apply what you have learned to your own style.

Habits to avoid

The following is a list of the speech habits considered most annoying. As you read through it, think about which of these habits you might have.

Mumbling

People who mumble are annoying and difficult and sometimes impossible to understand. If you pay attention to them, you will notice that they barely open their mouths or move their tongues. They don't articulate consonants. Their speech is lacking in energy. They swallow words or run them together, leaving the listener to wonder what on earth they said.

To correct mumbling, you must:

Open your mouth to let sound escape.

Energize your tongue to articulate consonants.

Consonants are necessary to comprehension. Without them, speech loses its clarity.

Initial consonants are seldom the problem. Consonants that occur in the middle or at the end of a word are most frequently dropped.

One day, my eight-year old grandson came home from school and sat grumbling at the kitchen table. He was not a happy camper. He had missed a word on a spelling test, and since he is a very good speller who rarely misses a word, this was an issue for him. It turned out that the teacher had asked for the word "computer."

The word my grandson heard was "commuter," which he spelled correctly. To his way of thinking, he was being penalized for something the teacher had done wrong and he was quite vocal about it. If the teacher had articulated the consonant "p," I believe my grandson would have spelled computer correctly and we would all have had a much nicer day.

Commuter. - - - Computer.

A couple in Baltimore heard over their local radio station that there was to be a "Paul Harvey Festival" at the fairgrounds. Since they were great fans of Paul Harvey, they looked forward to hearing him speak and possibly having the opportunity to meet him. When the day arrived, they drove to the fairgrounds only to find the parking lot filled with recreational vehicles. They were puzzled until they read the sign above the parking lot: "Fall RV Festival!"

Paul Harvey. - - - Fall RV.

I doubt that they found the error amusing.

In a business situation misunderstandings such as this can be very serious.

Consonants carry the strength of the word. They must be pronounced clearly.

Dropping syllables

Consistently dropping syllables can seriously affect your professional image. The clarity and effectiveness with which you speak determines how seriously people take you. Each syllable in a word is there to be pronounced.

There are innumerable words in which syllables are frequently dropped. Note these few examples and others throughout this chapter.

reglar	*for*	regular
comtable	*for*	comfortable
particly	*for*	particularly
probly	*for*	probably

When George Bush was president, Dan Quayle often referred to him as Present Bush! I think that if Mr. Quayle likes the title of President, he should learn how to pronounce it!

President - - - Present

Consistently dropping syllables can seriously affect your professional image. Listen to others speak. Notice how often people drop consonants and how it weakens their speech.

Fading

Some time ago I heard a minister deliver a sermon in which only the first part of each sentence was audible. The last half of each sentence completely faded away so that his message was lost to the congregation. As he reached the high point of his sermon, he proclaimed dramatically,

> *"And the most important point for you to remember is that ......"*

The congregation never heard the important message that was meant to inspire them.

How many times have you missed the point being made because the last half of a sentence faded into an unintelligible mumble? You can avoid this habit if you sustain the energy in your voice until you've completed the sentence.

Dr. June Johnson

If something is important enough to be said, it's important enough to be heard.

Hesitating

A hesitation is a gap between words that belong together that occurs in the middle of a phrase or sentence. It disrupts the flow of thought and makes you sound unsure of what you are saying. A gap is not to be confused with a pause, which is used to clarify the meaning of what is being said.

Gaps interrupt the flow of a thought or idea and create the impression that you're not sure of what you're saying.

> *"I'd like to...uh...maybe...take my...uh ...dog with...me...when I...go."*

Al Gore is boring as a speaker because he uses far too many gaps in his sentences. Sentences need to flow smoothly with pauses used to phrase and heighten the meaning behind the words, not gaps that drain the energy.

"Upspeak"

A habit that's becoming increasingly common is upspeak. In upspeak, statements of fact are turned into questions.

> *We should take the road less traveled?*

> *There is no point in negotiating?*

When a statement of fact is turned into a question, the speaker seems to be asking "Do you agree with me?" Although upspeak is usually intended as a polite way to encourage agreement, it simply makes the speaker sound unsure.

What this country needs is a few good men?

George Bush used upspeak frequently, which may have contributed to the press labeling him as a wimp. A statement of fact requires a downturn at the end of a sentence.

What this country needs is a few good men.
Period.

Rate of speech

Do you speak faster than people can listen? Is it because your inner motor is running too fast? Or, is it because you are nervous? In either case, take a deep breath and slow down.

Information delivered at too fast a pace is difficult to absorb. It is possible to speak 250 or more words a minute, but the average person can easily comprehend only about 150 to 180 words a minute.

When you speak too fast there is no time for inflection, phrasing or word stress - all necessary for interpretation. If you have been told you speak too fast, take heed and slow down.

Talking at people

Talk **to** people - - not **at** them.

If your voice is loud, harsh or strident you're using too much vocal pressure. Not only is it unpleasant to listen to, it is harmful to the voice because of the pressure it puts on the vocal folds. No one likes the feeling of being assaulted by the voice. People are more receptive to a voice that is pleasant and well modulated.

On the other side of the coin, if the voice is so soft that people have to strain to hear what is being said, they will lose interest.

Using fillers

As with hesitations, fillers create the impression that you either don't have much to say or are not sure of what you're saying. Fillers are the "garbage" words such as:

ya know	ya see
like	ya unnerstan
really	uh
-er	um

Filler words clutter speech and fill time without contributing a thing to communication.

One radio station runs a contest in which callers have to talk for 20 seconds about a given topic without using "uh." You might want to try timing yourself, with "uh" or any of the above words.

Place your tape recorder beside your telephone and turn it on whenever you are on the phone. Forget that it's there. You'll not only hear how often you use fillers, but also how you sound to others.

Your speech habits are extremely important when you're on the telephone because there is no body language to help listeners interpret your meaning. They can only hear what you say, and the way you say it.

Personal checklist

Now that you have read about the habits you want to avoid, it is time to hear your voice. Tape a three minute reading of something that has interest for you. Listen to it with a critical ear. Check the habits below that you feel apply to you. Identifying them is the first step toward eliminating them.

- ☐ Mumbling

- ☐ Dropping Consonants

- ☐ Dropping Syllables

- ☐ Fading away

- ☐ Up speaking

☐ Speeding

☐ Hesitating

☐ Using fillers

Summary:

Understand your voice.

Listen to others.

Purchase and use a tape recorder.

Identify habits to be eliminated.

Establish your goals.

Say what you mean and mean what you say.

Chapter Three

DEVELOPING YOUR PERSONAL STYLE

*Speech finely framed
delighteth the ear.*

2 Maccabees 15:39

S tyle is a combination of techniques that make your speech interesting. Just as you bring your personal style into the way you dress, you want to create a personal style in the way you speak. There are no hard or fast rules; it's a very personal thing with no right or wrong.

You can develop your own personal style by incorporating the following techniques into the way you speak.

Inflection

The voice that lacks inflection speaks on one tone and sounds robotic, monotonous and dull. The speaking voice has a natural range of 5 to 8 tones. It is important to use these tones as you speak to add variety, interest and color to your voice and what you are saying.

Both Henry Kissinger and Robert Dole speak in monotones. Their speech is completely devoid of inflection.

In "My Fair Lady," Henry Higgins used a xylophone to show Eliza Doolittle how to develop inflection. He first played the sentence below on the xylophone and then had Eliza imitate the pitches. It was the most direct way to bring inflection into her voice. You can do the same on the piano with any sentence. As you read the sentences, notice how the voice rises and falls.

kind   come.

       let

How   of you to   me

As you read the following sentences, notice how the voice naturally rises and falls.

    love

        go

I'd   to   with you.

When   you?

       see

   will I

Once you get the idea, try using inflection with other sentences. It adds to your personal style, making you sound so much more interesting than if you say everything on one pitch.

Pacing

Interesting speakers vary the pace at which they speak
Sentences delivered at the same rate of speed are dull
and uninteresting. Vary the rate at which you speak.
Pick up speed to make a specific point more important or
dramatic or speak at a slower pace to stress an important
point. The important thing is to use variety as you speak.

To hold a listener's attention, lower your voice and vary your speed.

Pauses

Pauses in speech are like commas in writing - they help separate thoughts, emphasize certain points and keep things in logical order. Properly timed pauses also help you create more important or quiet points.

Many speakers avoid pauses because they fear silence. Pauses of a few seconds can seem like an eternity to someone who is uncomfortable with them. Avoid the tendency to fill the silence with the fillers we discussed earlier. (uh, um, like, really, ya' know, -er)

There are natural pauses and planned pauses. Natural pauses usually go unnoticed. They occur naturally and make it easier for the listener to follow what is being said. Planned pauses are used to heighten interest in what you're saying and make your speech more interesting. With planned pauses that are dramatic, always maintain eye contact so the audience knows you have not lost your train of thought.

A dramatic pause can be a powerful way to hold the attention of your audience. I once heard a minister open his sermon with a very strong and dramatic, **"JESUS CHRIST!"** after which he paused for what seemed like an eternity. He stared intently and then, pointing his finger at the congregation, said in a soft, intense voice, "**lived and died for you.**" That was the most effective use of a pause that I have ever heard.

Phrasing

Phrasing is the natural division of ideas that allows for interpretation and enhances the meaning of what is being said.

Phrases are defined by pauses and serve to clarify ideas, move from one point to another and hold the listener's attention. The underlying meaning of a sentence or statement can be altered or changed simply by the way it is phrased.

Word stress

Word stress is an important technique that can alter and enhance the meaning of a sentence. It enables you to emphasize the point you're making and give it greater clarity. Stressed words are necessary in every sentence you say. If nothing is stressed, the meaning may be unclear.

The following exercise uses a simple sentence to demonstrate this point.

Speak each sentence stressing the highlighted word. Notice how each stress changes the meaning of the sentence.

Mary was concerned about the test she was about to take. (not her sister)

Mary **was** concerned about the test she was about to take. (but no longer is)

Mary was **concerned** about the test she was about to take. (but not necessarily fearful)

Mary was concerned about the **test** she was about to take. (and possibly her grade)

Mary was concerned about the test **she** was about to take. (not someone else)

Mary was concerned about the test she was **about** to take. (not the one she had taken)

Mary was concerned about the test she was about to **take.** (not give)

This is a technique used by actors as they study the interpretation of their lines. If you are preparing a presentation, practice the sentences this way to find the clearest and most effective interpretation.

Energy

Energy is the vitality and enthusiasm you bring to your voice and is not to be confused with volume.

Volume is the decibel level at which you speak.

Energy is the intensity in the voice.

It is the difference between speaking **at** people (volume) and **to** people (energy).

Whether you're speaking with your full voice or softly, energy is a vital element. Supporting the voice from the diaphragm enables you to use a stronger, more energetic voice without pushing or forcing.

To improve your energy level, practice the exercises for diaphragmatic breathing presented later in this book.

Variety

Variety is the sum of all the above points. Study, listen and practice each one of them to create your personal speaking style.

Summary:

Understand what constitutes style.

Use the techniques that suit your personality.

Develop a comfortable style that fits you.

Chapter Four

BREATHING

The foundation of good speech

Whatever we conceive well, we express clearly and words flow with ease.

Boileau

A ll vocal improvement begins with the basics. The basics for developing a successful speaking voice are:

diaphragmatic breathing for power

resonance for warmth

articulation for clarity

body language for authority

In the next chapters you will be learning and practicing the skills necessary to develop a more powerful speaking voice. As you practice each new skill, keep in mind that all change feels unnatural and uncomfortable at first.

Although you have been breathing since you were born, you have probably not paid much attention to it. You need to be aware of the two types of breathing - diaphragmatic and costal.

Diaphragmatic breathing uses the full lung capacity while costal (or high chest) breathing uses only the upper half or third of the lung capacity.

Diaphragmatic breathing is the foundation of speech, the support that provides the power behind the voice. By using the full lung capacity, your body provides the energy that gives your voice its depth and authority and enables you to project with ease. It also keeps the voice from rising in pitch when you are upset or nervous.

Diaphragmatic breathing also enables you to breathe quietly, helps to control nerves and improves your health by removing dead air from your lungs. If you have ever studied voice or a wind instrument, or participated in meditation, yoga, or tai chi, you are already familiar with diaphragmatic breathing. It is an integral part of each of these disciplines.

Costal (or chest) breathing, uses only a portion of the lung capacity causing the chest and shoulders to rise with inhalation and fall with exhalation. By limiting the intake of air it deprives the voice of support and pushes the voice into the throat. The result is a higher pitch vocal strain and a voice that lacks depth and the ability to project.

Think back to your last physical when the doctor asked you to take a deep breath to listen to your lungs. Was your inhalation audible and did your shoulders and chest rise? If so, you were breathing from the chest, not the diaphragm.

First, relax!

Use the following techniques to help you relax.

> Stand tall, with both feet planted squarely on the floor, under your hips.
>
> Raise your arms and stretch as high as possible.
>
> Drop the arms and rotate the shoulders backward and forward to loosen them.
>
> Move your head slowly from side to side to relax the neck.

Swing your upper torso from side to side, gently, to loosen the waist muscles.

Stretch the back throat muscles with deep yawns, letting the jaw drop completely

Close your eyes and breathe deeply several times as you inhale and exhale slowly.

You should be feeling very relaxed. Whenever you experience tension, practice this routine to help you reduce the tension.

One of my clients was very nervous about a meeting she had scheduled with her boss. She knew that it could become confrontational and didn't want to start out by being nervous. She used the relaxation technique and the meeting went so well that her boss complimented her on how well she handled it.

How diaphragmatic breathing works

To develop diaphragmatic breathing, you need to reprogram the muscles surrounding your rib cage to expand as you breathe. When these muscles expand, the lungs automatically inflate like a balloon and pull the air into them.

To experience the muscle movement involved in diaphragmatic breathing, sit or stand tall and gasp as though taken by surprise. Notice how your midsection expands and how the lungs are filled as you gasp. This is the muscle movement that you use to breathe from the diaphragm. Gasp a few times to familiarize yourself with how it feels.

Cough or sneeze a few times. The muscle movement in your midsection is the same muscle movement used in diaphragmatic breathing.

The steps listed below will help you start on the road to strengthening these muscles.

Stand tall, lift your shoulders to your ears, roll them back and let them fall naturally into place.

Place your hands on the sides of your rib cage, just above your waist.

Push against your hands until you feel the rib cage expanding. Your rib cage probably won't expand very much at first but will gain flexibility as you practice.

Pretend your rib cage is an accordion. Move it in and out until you feel the muscles around the ribcage gaining in flexibility. By practicing this exercise daily throughout the day you will strengthen these muscles and develop the habit of breathing from the diaphragm at all times.

If you are having difficulty with this exercise, practice it lying on the floor. Breathe deeply and, as you inhale and exhale, notice how your midriff rises and falls and your shoulders and chest remain stationary. This is the same movement you should be experiencing when doing the exercise in an upright position. All movement takes place in your midsection.

If you are still having trouble, begin your practice by lying on the floor. As you breathe deeply, notice how your midriff rises and falls. This is the same exercise just described, except in a prone position.

How to practice diaphragmatic breathing:

Assume the posture above, with shoulders back and chest high. Exhale all the air from your lungs.

Expand your rib cage and feel the lungs inflate.

Gradually exhale the air with a slow, pressurized, steady stream of air as though blowing through a straw.

Count (silently) as you exhale.

Time yourself to measure your improvement as you repeat the exercise. Twenty or twenty-five seconds is sufficient. The purpose behind this exercise is to develop the strength in the muscles around your rib cage by reprogramming them, not to see how long you can stretch your breath.

For a variation on the above, inhale and substitute the blowing with hissing as you exhale slowly. Sssssssssssssss. Alternate the two exercises.

When to practice

Luckily, this is a skill you can practice at any time during the day. Think of all the "lost times" you have, such as standing in line at the post office, grocery store or bank. You can practice deep breathing during those times. No one will be the wiser and breathing from the diaphragm will become a habit before you know it.

Summary:

Control your breath and you control your voice.

Diaphragmatic breathing enables you to:

speak with authority

project your voice

control your nerves

Practice frequently throughout the day.

Good diaphragmatic power comes with . . .

PRACTICE, PRACTICE, PRACTICE

Chapter Five

ARTICULATION

The key to good diction

Speak clearly if you speak at all;
carve every word before you let it fall.

Oliver Wendell Holmes

A rticulation is the meat and potatoes, the bread and butter of speech. According to the dictionary, articulation is, "The power of speech ... divided into clear and distinct words."

Well-articulated speech calls for:

> Energized consonants.
>
> Sentences that flow smoothly, using pauses not gaps.
>
> Pronunciation of all syllables.
>
> Articulation at ending consonants.
>
> Consistent pronunciation of vowels.
>
> Energy maintained throughout the entire sentence.

How articulation works

The lips and tongue are the articulators that determine how clearly you speak. They need to be actively involved in all speech. Since consonants carry the meaning of what you're saying and are necessary to comprehension, it is important that they be articulated in a clear and precise manner.

It takes energy to speak with good articulation. You can have the most beautiful voice in the world but if the consonants are missing or sluggish, the beautiful voice will have little effect.

When I was in elementary school, we always recited the Pledge of Allegiance before class. For a long time I thought we were pledging our allegiance: "... to the republic for Richard stands."

When I first began to use voice mail, the message from the operator always sounded as though she was telling me to "enter your tentative number." It was some time before I realized that what she was asking for was my "ten digit number."

Where to begin

You begin by opening your mouth and moving your jaw as you speak. To check how much you should open your mouth, practice speaking in front of a mirror. Pay particular attention to how much separation there is between your teeth. If there is little or none, you are probably mumbling.

To give you an idea about how much space you need to speak clearly, place your forefinger in your mouth without touching your lips or teeth. This is how much you should be opening your mouth.

Keep your jaw relaxed so that your mouth moves easily and people can hear and understand your words.

How to practice

How effectively you use your tongue and lips when articulating consonants determines how well you speak. The exercises in this chapter are designed to develop agility in your tongue and lips. As you say them, **exaggerate** the consonants. The more you exaggerate in practice, the sooner your articulation will improve and you will be able to relax when saying them.

Consonants

There are two types of consonants - voiced and unvoiced. Voiced consonants are vocalized, meaning they have sound. Unvoiced consonants are whispered. Since unvoiced consonants have no sound of their own, they require the addition of a vowel sound to be heard.

Several of the consonants are cognates, paired according to the action of the tongue and lips. For example: B, said by bringing the lips together to articulate, is vocalized, while P, also said by bringing the lips together, is whispered or unvoiced. Unvoiced consonants are called plosives.

The following chart indicates the pairing of the voiced and unvoiced consonants according to the way they are pronounced. As you say the following pairs, be sure to say the voiced consonants with sound and the unvoiced ones only as a plosive. Notice the tongue action for each pair and the difference in sound.

Volume is not important. They can be said softly as long as they are said with an energetic tongue.

Voiced		*Unvoiced*
b	lips together	p
d	tongue behind upper teeth	t
g	tongue lifted in back to soft palate	c (hard) k
v	teeth against lower lip	f
z	tongue against lower teeth	s (soft c)
zh (treasure)	tongue against side molars	ch (church)
gz (exist)	back of tongue raised followed by z	ks (explain)

The following words are paired according to the tongue action required to pronounce the consonants. Practice them in these pairs. Exaggerate each consonant. The more you exaggerate each consonant in practice, the sooner you will establish the habit of clearer, sharper speech.

Volume is not important. The words can be said softly, as long as they are said with energy. Once the habit of clear articulation is established, you can relax into pronouncing the words with less exaggeration.

EXERCISE WORDS

Voiced	*Unvoiced*	*Voiced*	*Unvoiced*
B	P	D	T
bark	park	dime	time
bump	pump	dent	tent
beach	peach	dock	tock
bob	pop	deed	teed
bees	peas	adder	latter
G	K (hard c)	V	F
glad	clad	vain	fain
gape	cape	vale	fail
gall	call	vault	fault
grape	crepe	prove	proof
league	leak	leave	leaf
NG	NK	Z	S(soft c)
sung	sunk	zeal	seal

Voiced	Unvoiced	Voiced	Unvoiced
thing	think	zink	sink
bring	brink	Zorro	sorrow
bang	bank	zipper	slipper
tang	tank	zoo	sue
ZH	CH	CZ	KS
treasure	church	exist	explain
casual	choose	exalt	extol
vision	check	exhort	extend
illusion	child	examine	expect
intrusion	chipper	exaggerate	expire

Commonly mispronounced words

The mispronunciation of vowels and the elimination of consonants and syllables are common problems. They are often the cause of misunderstandings. The following list represents a few of the words most commonly mispronounced. As you read through the list, check those you use frequently and may mispronounce. Practice saying them correctly. Make your own list of mispronounced words as you listen to others speak.

Voiced	Unvoiced	Voiced	Unvoiced
Actual	Akchul	Library	Liberry
All right	Awright	Literally	Li/rully
Always	Aw-weez	Mayor	Mare
Any	Iny	Midst	Mist
Asked	Axed	Million	Miyun
Attentive	Atenive	Mirror	Mirra
Ball game	Bawgame	Model	Mahdo
Because	Buhcuz	Nuclear	Nuclur
Center	Cenner	Older	Odor
Cold	Code	Particularly	Particly
Comparable	Compable	Perhaps	Praps
Could have	Cudda	Picture	Pitcher
Didn't	Dint	Plenty	Plenny
Etcetera	Eksetra	Probably	Probly
Elementary	Elemenary	Pneumonia	Amonia

Voiced	Unvoiced	Voiced	Unvoiced
February	Febry	Poem	Pome
Gentle	Gennel	President	Present
Get	Git	Realtor	Relator
Geography	Jogafee	Recognize	Recanize
Going to	Gonna	Regular	Regler
Goodbye	Guhbye	Secretary	Secetary
Hardly	Harly	Specifically	Pacifically
Help	Hep	Tired	Tard
Hospital	Hospitoo	Twenty	Twenny
Hundred	Hunnert	Understand	Unnerstand
Important	Impornt	William	Wiyum
Interesting	Inneresing	Window	Winnow

Problem consonant "L"

One of the most mispronounced consonants in our
language is the L. Many people substitute a W for the L.
Words such as building sound like "biwding," and ball
game, "bawgame." If this is a problem for you, practice

saying the L by bringing the tip of the tongue to the hard surface behind the upper teeth. Relax your jaw and with a quick action of the tip of the tongue, say "la, la, la, la, la" several times until the tongue moves with ease. Use the same tongue action in the following words and sentences.

Practice words

Correct	Incorrect	Correct	Incorrect
Apple	Appoo	Trouble	Trouboo
Ball game	Baw game	William	Wiyum
Hospital	Hospitoo	Call you	Caw you
Simple	Simpoo	Tell you	Tehyou

Practice sentences

Lady luck lives a lively life.

Likable ladies are lovable.

Telling tall tales means trouble.

Luminous aluminum and voluminous linoleum.

Be likable, lovable and livable or you're liable to be leavable, left and lonesome.

Give me a little farm well tilled, a little barn well filled and a little wife well willed.

Clarice the classy clown clamored clumsily over the climbing clematis.

Willie cluttered the clothes in the clothes basket under the clothesline.

Problem consonant "T"

The consonant T is a problem because it's often pronounced as a D, especially when it occurs in the middle of a word. "Better" becomes "bedder". "Matter" becomes "madder." The initial T is seldom a problem. It's the T at the end of a word that is usually eliminated.

As with the L, the T is said by placing the tip of the tongue against the hard palate behind the upper teeth. Practice saying Tee, Tee, Tee, Tee, Tee, with a rapid, sharp tongue movement. Don't be afraid to exaggerate.

As you practice the following words, exaggerate all Ts with a sharp, explosive sound. Once you've established the habit, you will settle into saying the Ts more naturally.

Better	Chatter	Internet
Letter	Matter	Water
Bitter	Center	Interest
Lettuce	Pretty	Waiter
Twenty	Clatter	Saturday
Sweater	Let us	Suited

Canchu, Dinchu

When "you" follows a word ending in T, the tendency is to pronounce "you" as "chou" or "chuh," as in "wanchu," "wanchuh," "dinchou" or "dinchuh." The T at the end of the first word should be pronounced distinctly and followed with a clear Y, not a CH.

Want you - - Didn't you

Also, avoid substituting "yuh" or "ya" for "you." Practice saying the following.

Want you	Can't you
Aren't you	Won't you
Didn't you	Don't you
Sent you	Meet you
Greet you	Let you

Consonant confusion

Lazy or eliminated consonants cause problems in comprehension. The following list represents a sample of the words commonly that can cause misunderstandings because of missing consonants.

Scene	Seeing
Winter	Winner

Rampant	Rapid
Boring	Born
Cold	Code
Boat	Bode
Late	Lay
Latter	Ladder
Computer	Commuter
Said	Set
Inter	Inner

Tongue twisters

Tongue twisters are an excellent way to sharpen your articulation. Singers, actors and television personalities use these regularly. Not only are they useful, they are fun.

How to practice tongue twisters

Select one of the tongue twisters below and begin by saying it slowly, articulating every consonant. Don't be afraid to overdo it at this point. Tape yourself and listen for consonants that are sloppy or eliminated. When you are able to say the sentence accurately, gradually increase your speed. When you stumble or eliminate a consonant, slow down and repeat the sentence.

Your goal is to be able to say each sentence as rapidly as possible, pronouncing each consonant clearly and crisply. Volume is not important. Saying them softly is effective as long as they are said with energy.

Twisters to twist your tongue

A tutor who tooted a flute tried to tutor two tutors to toot. Said the two to the tutor, is it harder to toot or to tutor two tutors to toot.

Betty bought some butter but the butter Betty bought was bitter. So Betty bought some better butter to make the bitter butter better. But the bitter butter Betty bought makes the better butter bitter.

Theopholus Thistle, the thistle-sifter, sifted a sieve of unsifted thistles. If Theopholus Thistle the thistle-sifter, sifted a sieve of unsifted thistles, where is the sieve of unsifted thistles Theopholus Thistle, the thistle-sifter, sifted?

If she stops at the shop where I stop and if she shops at the shop where I shop, then I shan't stop to stop at the shop where she stops to shop.

A big black bug bit a big black bear and the big black bear bled blood.

Moses supposes his toeses are roses. But Moses supposes erroneously. For Moses knowes his toeses aren't roses as Moses supposes his toeses to be.

A skunk stood on a stump. The stump thunk the skunk stunk and the skunk thunk the stump stunk.

A flea and a fly were caught in a flu. Said the flea to the fly, "What shall we do?" Said the fly to the flea, "Let us fly!" Said the flea to the fly, "Let us flee!" So the flea and the fly flew through a flaw in the flu.

Vowels

Vowels are as important to speech as consonants. Mispronounced vowels and sloppy consonants are responsible for many misunderstandings. One of the challenges in the English language are the many different pronunciations of single vowels and vowel combinations.

When I was Professor of Voice at the Eastern Illinois University, one of my responsibilities was to teach vocal diction to voice majors. English was their native language, but they still had to learn to pronounce words correctly so they could be understood as they sang. Many had regional accents that turned sentences like "When can I get it?" into something that sounded like "Win kin ah git it?" They had to work to develop a consistent pronunciation of vowel sounds.

In the English language, there are only five written vowels, a, e, i, o, u, but there are ten vowel sounds.

ooh	to
oh	no

oo	took
aw	saw
ah	fond
a	apple
uh	up
eh	said
ih	sit
ee	me

The vowel or vowel combination in a word does not always correspond to the sound we associate with that vowel. In other words, there can be a number of different spellings for one vowel sound or vowel combination.

Take the combination "ough." It can be pronounced six different ways – bought, lough, rough, though, thought and through. Is it any wonder that English is a difficult language to learn?

The following list shows some of the different pronunciations for each of the vowel sounds.

ooh	food, truth, tune, shoe, grew
oh	boat, wrote, known, phone
oo	look, should, put, bull

aw	Paul, tall, thought, lawn
ah	father, bother, plot, fond
a	apple, and, sad, anger, trample
uh	up, some, trouble, love
eh	said, any, plenty, head
ih	myth, business, pretty, since
ee	seem, people, believer, dream

Pay attention to how you shape your mouth as you pronounce the vowel sounds. Your tongue should be as flat on the floor of your mouth as the vowel sound allows. In other words, for the first five vowels (oo, oh, oo, aw and ah) the lips should be rounded and the tongue flat on the floor of your mouth. For the next two vowels (a and uh), the mouth should be more open and tongue in a slightly higher position. For the last three (eh, ih, and ee), the tongue is higher in the mouth and the lips more open but not spread.

As you go through the following words, pay particular attention to the position of your tongue, the shape of your lips and the space inside your mouth.

| ooh | moon | boon | room | doom | wound |
| oh | moan | bone | roam | dough | woe |

oo	hood	bush	could	look	wood
aw	mall	bought	ought	dawn	wall
ah	mom	bond	romp	don	wand
a	man	band	ranch	brand	trance
uh	done	love	plush	fudge	lush
eh	men	bend	rend	dent	went
ih	mint	bin	rim	dint	wind
ee	mean	bean	real	deal	wee

Diphthongs

A diphthong is a sound in speech that begins with one vowel sound and moves into a second sound - a semi-vowel within the same syllable. The first vowel is the principal sound and is sustained longer, while the second vowel sound is short.

For example, the letter "I" is pronounced "eye." To pronounce it correctly requires two sounds. The principal sound "ah" and the secondary sound "ih." "My" begins with "maaah" and a quick "ih" - maaahih. If you stress or linger on the second vowel sound, the word sounds like "maheeee." On the other hand, if you eliminate the second vowel sound, it sounds like "maaah."

As you say the following diphthongs, the jaw should be relaxed and the mouth round. Avoid spreading your lips as you move to the second vowel sound. Let your tongue change the sound.

(<u>ah</u>ih)	my	sigh	time
	write	side	rhyme
(<u>aw</u>ih)	boy	coin	royal
	joist	foil	choice
(<u>ay</u>ih)	fame	same	train
	plain	blame	delay
(<u>ah</u>oo)	found	loud	cloud
	about	town	allow

Stress the underlined sound and move only the tongue to say the second sound.

(<u>aaah</u>ih)	mind	nine	might
	sign	divine	night
(<u>aaaw</u>ih)	moist	join	point
	employ	annoy	loyal
(<u>aaay</u>ih)	may	main	mail
	knave	made	blade
(<u>aaah</u>oo)	mound	mouth	now
	bound	gown	down

Summary:

Good articulation requires energy.

Pronounce all consonants.

Establish consistent vowel sounds.

Check your Ls and Ts.

Practice the tongue twister daily.

ARTICULATE, ARTICULATE, ARTICULATE!

EXAGGERATE, EXAGGERATE, EXAGGERATE!

ENERGIZE, ENERGIZE, ENERGIZE!

Chapter Six

RESONANCE

The warmth in your voice

*There are tones in the voice
that mean more than words.*

Robert Frost

Dr. June Johnson

R esonance is the "hum" in the voice that gives it the warm, rich sound that is pleasant to hear. The body is full of sounding chambers called resonating cavities They include the head, sinuses, mouth, throat and chest, all of which are essential to producing resonance. If you use these cavities or chambers well, you improve the quality of your voice, establish good vocal habits and eliminate vocal fatigue.

Nasality, on the other hand, is caused by lowering the soft palate so that most of the air is exhaled through the nose rather than the mouth. The result is the concentration of the resonance in the nose, closing off all the other resonating cavities. This causes a twang in the voice and is usually identified with people who whine.

An example of good use of resonance is the actor, James Earl Jones. With his deep and vibrant voice, he is thrilling to listen to. When he speaks, you are hearing resonance at its richest. But James Earl Jones was not born with that wonderful sounding voice.

As a child, he stuttered so badly he tried to avoid speaking. With determination and practice, however, he not only overcame the stuttering but went on to develop the resonant voice that has become his trademark.

Actor Richard Burton also had a wonderfully resonant quality in his voice. When he was young, he spent hours in the hills of his native Wales practicing projection and resonance.

"Placing" the voice for resonance

Concert and opera singers train for years to "place" the voice to expand the vocal range, increase flexibility, project with ease and maintain a healthy voice. Without proper placement a singer would be unable to sustain the voice through a full performance. The same technique will benefit you as a speaker.

"Placing" means placing the voice in the mask or front of the face. This helps you project your voice and avoid the hoarseness and fatigue that comes with speaking from the throat. It also will eliminate the breathy sound that sometimes occurs from the lack of support and poor placement.

How to "place" the voice

The voice is "placed" by vibrating the resonating cavities in the body with a hum. These cavities include the sinuses, head, nose, mouth, throat and chest. The body is the sounding board or instrument for the voice, just as the piano is for the pianist. Play on it!

The following exercises are designed to develop the hum, or resonance, in your voice. As you follow these steps, keep the lips and jaw free of tension. Any tightness in either will cause the voice to be tight.

> Relax.

> Bring the lips together and hum softly until you begin to feel your lips tingle.

Place your thumb and forefinger lightly on the bridge of your nose and repeat the hum. Feel the vibration or buzz in the nose. (This is probably the cheapest buzz you will ever experience!)

Increase the volume of the hum until you feel your lips buzz.

Place your hand on your chest as you hum and feel the vibrations in the chest cavity.

Move up and down the scale as you hum and pretend you are a siren or race car. Use as wide a vocal range as possible. This will increase your range of inflection as well.

How to practice

Now that you understand how to "place" your voice, it is time for exercises to develop your resonance.

Each of the words and sentences in the following exercises is filled with m's and n's. These sounds produce the hum necessary to establish resonance. As you repeat the words and sentences, linger on the m's and n's until you feel a buzz in your face and a tingle in your lips.

Once you feel the buzz, take care to shape your mouth as you pronounce the vowel.

To give you an example, take the word "momentum." As you say it, linger on each m and n until you feel the buzz -- mmmommmmennntummm. It's important to keep the buzz. By lengthening the two consonants in this way you will increase the resonance in your voice. As you open your mouth for the vowel sounds, maintain the resonance so that it carries through the entire word.

To give you an example, take the word "momentum." As you say it, exaggerate and linger on each m and n until you feel the buzz – mmmommmennntummm. Maintain the buzz as you open your mouth to say the vowel. Be sure to carry the hum through the vowel sound. Keep the inside of your mouth as round as the vowel sound permits to maintain the full resonance. Closing up the space inside the mouth will cause you to sound nasal.

Practice each of the words below always working for the buzz. When you feel the buzz repeat the word three times, running it together to create one word, like this:

Mmommenntumm/mmommenntumm/mmommenntumm

Exaggerate the hum with each m and n and carry it into the vowels.

Momentum	Meaning
Mimosa	Minimum
Mammoth	Moonbeam
Nonsense	Noontime
Nimble	Humming

Use the same technique of lingering on the hum sounds in the following sentences:

Many men make money moving memos.

(Ex. Mmmannny mmmennn mmmake
mmmonnney mmmoving mmmemmmos)
Nine unknown men in Maine.

I roam from Nome to Rome and home.

Memorable moments are meaningful to me.

Singing means bringing resonance into my tone.

The rain in Spain stays mainly on the plain.

When to practice

I recommend that these exercises not be practiced during the "lost times" I mentioned for breathing. You'll provoke some strange stares if you do. Practice them when you are alone and free to exaggerate the humming. Many of my clients tell me they practice them while in the car where you now doubt have a great deal of lost time!

Summary:

Place the voice in the mask of the face.

Use the hum to develop resonance.

And don't forget to

EXAGGERATE, EXAGGERATE, EXAGGERATE!

ENERGIZE, ENERGIZE, ENERGIZE!!!

PRACTICE, PRACTICE, PRACTICE!

Chapter Seven

BODY LANGUAGE

The Silent Voice

The body is the message.

Julius Fast

B ody language is the oldest, most trusted language in the world. It was around long before the spoken word and accounts for 55% of what we communicate, while the voice accounts for 38% and the words for only 7%.

What is body language?

Body language is the involuntary, unconscious language of communication while speech is the intelligent process. Every movement, every glance, every gesture you make says something about you and reveals more than you may want to reveal. Increasing your understanding of body language enables you to use yours more effectively and to read the body language of others.

When body language does not match what the voice is saying, communication is misleading and confusing. Body and vocal language are the Siamese twins of speech.

Understanding body language

Before you even open your mouth, people are making assumptions about you based on your non-verbal cues. Are you to be taken seriously or dismissed? Are you warm and friendly or stiff and distant?

Do you smile easily, or do you scowl? Do you walk with assurance and confidence when you enter a room, or do you slip in hoping you won't be noticed? Do you meet people easily, or do you have difficulty in new situations? These are only a few of the things that your silent voice, or body language, reveals about you.

How to use body language effectively

The first step to understanding and controlling your body language is to recognize what your non-verbal cues are saying. Your eyes, facial expression, gestures, posture and walk all tell who you are. Gaining control of these physical mannerisms is as important to your message as the message itself.

The eyes

The eyes have it. There is a wonderful old Irish song that goes "When Irish eyes are smiling, all the world seems bright and gay." Take these words to heart because the world does seem bright and gay when you meet smiling eyes.

Your eyes show how you feel about yourself and have a direct bearing on how others feel about you. People are constantly interpreting what they read in other's eyes. How often have you heard the expression, "I could see it in her eyes?" or "Did you see those shifty eyes?"

The Greeks considered the eyes to be the mirror of your heart, capable of expressing a wide range of emotions - love, hate, anger, joy, sadness, anguish, jealousy or disappointment, to name just a few. The most pleasant of these emotions is found in eyes that smile. Smiling gives eyes a vitality that indicates friendliness, sincerity and interest. Smiles are catching and invite people to relate positively to you.

People in power know how to use their eyes to maintain control. They master looks that convey authority, confidence, warmth or concern. They know better than to look down or look nervously around a room since that indicates disinterest or insecurity.

When speaking with an individual, look directly into the eyes. One of the tricks used by John F. Kennedy was to alternate the eye he was looking into by moving his gaze from one eye to the other. It kept his expression lively and gave the impression that he was very interested in what was being said.

Direct eye contact should be maintained only about 70 to 75% of the time. By glancing away occasionally you avoid intense staring that makes people uncomfortable.

When speaking before a group, let your eyes sweep around the room to include everyone. Audiences want to feel that you are speaking directly to them. Avoid looking over their heads, at the ceiling, off to the side or concentrating your attention on only a few individuals.

Keep your eyes vital and alive. Eyes that are dead and lacking in expression are referred to as fish eyes. They have the same cold , lifeless look as the eyes of a dead fish and can be very disconcerting.

During recent corporate downsizing, I worked with a number of clients who needed help preparing for job interviews. Several were middle-aged and had not interviewed for a job since graduating from college. Understandably, the idea of going for a job interview was a very uncomfortable one for them.

One particular gentleman referred to me by an outreach firm came for help on polishing his interview skills. Although he was thoroughly qualified and experienced in his field, he'd had several interviews and never received an offer. It didn't take long to identify his problem.

In our sessions we used role-playing to simulate interviews. As the interviewer, I asked him why he thought my company should hire him and, more particularly, what he would be able to bring to my company if I were to hire him.

Although he spoke knowledgeably about his subject, his body was very stiff with his hands clasped tightly in front of him. His face and eyes were expressionless with no trace of a smile. He never once took his eyes from me the entire time he was speaking. And he used "I" much too frequently. The result: I was so uncomfortable listening to him that I heard very little of what he was saying.

It was pretty obvious why he had never been offered a job. He came across as being a very rigid man with no sense of humor. There was no evidence of enthusiasm for the job and he demonstrated that his main concern was for himself. Also, his steady stare displayed an insensitivity to others that would cause a prospective employer to wonder if others would be comfortable working with him.

When I told him my reaction to his interview, he was not particularly happy, but he did agree to try to make some changes. We reenacted the interview a number of times until he began to relax enough to smile as he spoke and keep his eyes friendly and interested.

I also suggested he lean forward to show interest, make a few gestures with his hands and remove most of the "I" statements from his remarks. It must have worked because he called a couple of weeks later to say he had secured a position and thanked me for my help.

Facial expression

The expression on your face has a direct bearing on the way you sound. If you look stern, you will sound stern. A smile produces an upbeat, positive sound to your voice. The animation that a smile brings to the face puts a vitality and energy into the voice that says "I'm happy to see you!"

To hear the difference the smile makes in your voice, tape yourself reading a few sentences. Smile as you read them. Then assume a dour expression and re-tape the sentences. Play the tape back and notice the difference in the voice quality of each. The "smiling voice" will have vitality and interest; the "frowning voice" will sound lifeless and dull.

A smile will also help you to hide any nervousness you might be feeling. When you have a pleasant expression on your face, you will to feel much more positive about yourself. So, keep smiling. Others will cath it!

Gestures

Gestures are as necessary to your speech as your words. Used effectively, they serve to highlight and emphasize the points you consider important. They should be large enough to be meaningful, but not so large as to be distracting. Meaningless gestures - those unrelated to what is being said - will only detract attention from your words and undermine your message.

A number of years ago I heard a professional speaker who had a most distracting habit. As she spoke, she constantly removed her glasses when stressing a point. She swept them high above her head, put them back on and repeated the motion every three or four minutes throughout her presentation. I found myself so fascinated (and distracted) by her gestures that by the time she had finished, I had no memory of what she had said.

"What do I do with my hands?" is probably the most frequent question I am asked in my workshops. Hand gestures are not difficult to control. A simple rule is to keep all movements natural and comfortable. Establish the habit because when you are excessively nervous you won't have the faintest idea what your hands are doing as you speak.

Dr. June Johnson

One of the suggestions I make in my workshops is to imagine yourself standing in front of a window that extends to your waist just above shoulder level. A mirror can also serve the same purpose.

As you are speaking, keep your gestures within this framework. You will be less tempted to flail them with large, sweeping gestures that say nothing. Never extend your hands above your shoulders unless there is a specific reason for doing so.

You can use your hands in many ways. The following suggestions offer several possibilities. Practice them until they feel natural. Once you are comfortable with these gestures, be sure to vary them as you speak. Repeating the same gesture over and over can be as distracting as gestures that are meaningless or too broad.

> Let both arms hang by your side. This may feel uncomfortable at first but that will become more comfortable with practice.

> Keep one hand down and the other at waist level.

> Hold both hands at waist height, using one or both to emphasize your point.

> Keep elbows free of your body, not clamped tightly to your waist or ribs.

> Hands should be relaxed and open.

The following gestures indicate tension and should be avoided:

Tight, clenched fists

Elbows pressed against the body

Meaningless repeated gestures

Chopping the air with your hands

Pointing or nodding your head

Fiddling with items in your hand

Pointing a finger

Nodding your head

Fiddling with items in your hand

Hand or hands on hips

Hands in pocket

Be particularly aware of pointing your finger to stress a point. Many people are offended when they see a finger pointed at them. Use the extended open hand instead. Videotape yourself to determine how you are using gestures.

Stance

Power lies with the person who appears confident and in control. How you carry yourself, enter a room, walk, sit, or shake hands contributes to the impression of confidence. Whether stepping on stage or entering a room for a meeting, conference or interview, make your entrance a strong one. Stand tall, shoulders back and head high, and walk with a good steady stride.

One of my clients, the successful owner of a small company, had the habit of standing with one ankle crossed over the other. When I pointed it out to her, she was amazed. He had no idea she was doing that. But the video camera didn't lie.

Although she was slender, the narrowness at her feet made her appear top heavy and slightly off balance. I found myself wondering if she was going to tip over. Fortunately, she did not. She has changed this habit.

To convey confidence and authority with your stance:

> Stand tall and act with confidence, whether you feel it or not.

> Place feet directly under hips, one foot slightly in front of the other.

> Balance your weight on balls of both feet.

> Hold your shoulders back and chest high.

> Enter a room with a stride that indicates confidence.

Move about easily, but refrain from excessive roaming.

When sitting, sit tall and lean forward, with arms resting on the table rather than in the lap.

Avoid slouching in the chair.

Summary:

Understand and control your body language.

Use your eyes to establish rapport.

Use gestures that support your words.

Learn to read the body language of others.

Develop confidence with positive body language.

Chapter Eight

PITCH

The music that can deepest reach and cure all ill, is cordial speech.

Ralph Waldo Emerson

W e have already discussed how important breathing, resonance and articulation are to developing a winning voice. The one aspect we have not touched on is the pitch or tonal level at which we speak.

Both Marilyn Monroe and Jackie Kennedy had high pitched, breathy voices that were very feminine but totally lacking in support. In contrast, Bob Dole and Henry Kissinger have such low pitched voices they often sound as though they are growling.

The high-pitched voice is a handicap for anyone in business. It is irritating and lacks authority. Although it is usually associated with women, I have worked with many men who have high-pitched voices.

At the beginning of his career, Tom Selleck spoke with an unusually high voice for a man of his height. He is now speaking at a much lower pitch. For those of you who play golf, listen to Jack Nicklaus.

His voice lacks support, causing him to speak from his throat. Whenever I watch the golf matches and hear him speak, I want to tell him, "Jack, you put your body into your swing, why don't you put your body into your voice?"

Katie Couric of the NBC Today show was coached to lower her voice to soften her delivery, which had been judged to be too harsh. I have had a number of clients who have come for help because they were tired of being asked: "Is your mother at home?"

Although pitch varies from person to person, finding the pitch level at which your voice is most comfortable and sounds the best is important. If you are unhappy with your pitch level or feel it does not reflect the real you, you can find your best level in a number of ways.

Take a small breath and, as you exhale, say "ah ha" as though you were surprised at something someone said. Then try "um-hum" with lips closed as though you were questioning something someone said. Both of these phrases will cause your voice to settle to its true pitch level, the level you want to work toward.

To determine the pitch level at which you are currently speaking, say in your natural voice range, "I am going to lower the sound of my voice." As you say the phrase move your voice into a singing tone at the same pitch level. This is the pitch level at which you are currently speaking. If it is a significantly different pitch level from the "ah-ha" or "um-hum," you will want to work toward matching your pitch to the pitch of the two phrases.

If your aim is to establish your voice at a lower pitch level, repeat the above sentence, lowering the pitch one tone each time you say it until you arrive at a pitch level close to "ah-ha" and "um-hum." If you think your voice is too low, reverse the exercise, gradually moving it, tone by tone, to a higher pitch. Experiment with this exercise until you arrive at the pitch level that sounds best in your voice. If you are not sure, ask your family or friends for their opinion.

If you have access to a piano, you can use it to help you find the pitch that sounds right in your voice in the same way that Henry Higgins used the xylophone. Match your spoken tone to the musical tone on the piano. Then follow the procedure in the exercise above by using the piano to move your voice up or down. The pitches on the piano will serve as your guide. However, a piano is not essential. You can easily accomplish the same result without one. It simply makes it a little easier.

When you arrive at that comfortable pitch level, use your tape recorder to establish it in your voice. Practice reading out loud using inflection, word stress, pauses and phrasing to make it as interesting as possible.

Summary:

Experiment with lowering or raising your pitch level to find your true pitch.

Avoid the voice that is breathy or pitched too high or too low.

Support your voice with diaphragmatic breathing to speak with authority.

Chapter Nine

PLATFORM SKILLS

Be sincere.
Be brief.
Be seated.

Franklin Delano Roosevelt

G ood speakers are not born, they are created. Like any other skill, effective speaking is learned. It takes preparation and practice.

Preparation

The first step in preparation is to research your subject thoroughly. The better you know your topic, the better your presentation will be. Your audience will sense immediately how thorough your knowledge is and whether you have a firm grip on your material.

In this section, all references to speaking will be referred to as "presentations" and all groups, regardless of size and affiliation, will be referred to as "the audience."

Set your goals

Let us imagine you've been asked to speak before a group. You have a topic and a date. Where do you go from here?

First, ask for flyers or brochures containing information on the organization and the event. Establish a clear understanding of the type of presentation and length of program they are expecting and the information the sponsors are looking for you as the speaker to provide.

Find out if the presentation is expected to:

Provide information or specific skills.

Be motivational or inspirational.

Provide humor and entertainment.

Know your audience

Once all the initial details have been arranged, it is time to learn about your audience. To make your talk relevant, you will need some background information on your audience.

You can save yourself much time and effort by preparing a detailed questionnaire. Ask for information you can use to customize your program. Request that it be returned to you at least a month in advance so you have adequate time to prepare.

Request the following information:

Expected attendance

Ratio of male to female attendees

Average age

Areas of a company or business represented

Management
Office Staff
Sales
Customer Service

Theme of the convention

Business areas represented
Geographical areas represented

Timely events that have occurred lately,
particularly humorous ones.

Hobbies and interests of the group if pertinent

Although all of your presentations should be treated as a
form of conversation, speaking before 1,000 people is a
different situation from speaking to a group of 40 or 50.
In a large group, your approach to your topic will be
more formalized and style of delivery much broader.
With a smaller group, a more conversational approach is
appropriate and will help you establish rapport.

Planning your presentation

Every speech has an opening, a middle and a closing.
There is a saying among speakers: "Tell them what
you're going to tell them. Tell them. Then tell them what
you've told them." In other words, tell them what they
can expect to hear, then provide them with the supporting
material and finally, summarize the important points you
want them to remember.

This is the A-B-A form that is as old as Greek Drama and
still found in art, music, literature and theater - (A)
Exposition; (B) Development; (A) Recapitulation.

Dr. June Johnson

Delivery

Your opening is the most important part of your speech. You establish your credibility from the moment you enter the stage or room. You set the tone with your opening words. Plan your opening to catch and hold the attention of the audience and establish rapport. Memorize it, be able to say it in your sleep and deliver it with vitality and enthusiasm. If you have a humorous story that is pertinent to your topic, include it.

Organize your ideas in a logical, comprehensive format or segment. Depending on the makeup of the audience, bring in illustrations and stories that are relevant, including their occupations or hobbies. In 1996, I used all the politicians running for office, not for political comment, but as examples of poor speaking skills. Every candidate needed help and my imitations brought laughs.

Cover each segment in detail and recap it briefly to strengthen your message before moving on to the next section. Keep transitions clear. Speak in a natural, conversational tone. Avoid words that are too big and sentences that are too long.

In closing, summarize your main points. Conclude with a memorable closing, no longer than a short paragraph, that you have memorized. It can be a quote that is particularly relevant or your own thought. The purpose of the closing is to leave the audience with something to think about and take home with them. If there's time, ask for questions, or make yourself available.

Practice, practice and more practice

There is no shortcut to speaking effectively. It takes practice and a lot of it. Never give a presentation without having fully rehearsed it.

Zig Ziglar, world-renowned speaker, admits he would not dream of giving a presentation without practicing, although he has probably already presented it hundreds of times! If he feels the need to practice before each presentation, then you should too. The more you do it, the better you will become.

Use your tape recorder frequently as you prepare. This is a good way to know how you sound and how well you have organized your material. As you listen, note what does and does not work, and be prepared to make changes to improve it.

Invite your family and/or a group of friends to listen to you. Treat it as though it were a professional presentation from start to finish. Encourage them to make comments and suggestions. (If they are like most family and friends, they will enjoy giving you their opinions!)

If it is difficult to get a group together, then create a pretend audience. Draw upon your acting ability and imagine a group sitting before you. After all, public speaking is a form of acting. Establish eye contact with the imaginary audience as you sweep the room with your eyes. Videotape this presentation. It's the fastest and surest way to find out what you need to do to improve.

Final details

Provide a copy of your bio or introduction in advance and discuss with the introducer how you want it to be read. A poor introduction can set a bad tone for your presentation.

Check the room where you will be presenting, paying particular attention to the seating arrangement. There are a number of recommended seating arrangements and you may not have control over them. If possible, request that seats in a divided room be angled toward the center whether the audience is sitting at tables or in chairs. This arrangement keeps those sitting in the far end seats from having to turn their heads to see you.

Test microphones, overhead projectors, markers - all the equipment you will be using. Make sure there are extra bulbs for projectors. There is nothing more frustrating or embarrassing than standing by while an assistant struggles to fix inoperative equipment.

It's show time!

The better you know your presentation, the more relaxed you will feel. All of your practice will pay off to secure your memory, reduce nerves and fear and promote a feeling of confidence.

Use a natural, conversational approach with an easy, direct, informal manner. Tell stories and use humor that's relevant to your subject, even though the topic may be serious. There is humor to be found in every situation and the audience will appreciate it. Self-deprecating humor helps the audience to identify with you and feel comfortable.

I have heard Mikki Williams, a well-known motivational speaker, several times and each time have been deeply moved by her presentation. She tells her life story with all the tragedy she has known, but balances it beautifully with humor that makes you laugh frequently.

Always look professional with your stance and bearing. Be aware of your body language and use gestures and mannerisms to emphasize, not undermine, your words.

If you are using notes, put them in outline form on 5" x 8" cards and refer to them as little as possible.

When using a script, use large print, double-spaced for easy reading. Print the words on the top two-thirds of each page and slide the pages from left to right (or right to left) rather than flipping them.

Know your material so thoroughly that you only need to glance down occasionally. The audience needs to see your eyes, not the top of your head.

Keep in mind that every great speech motivates, educates and entertains and you'll be successful. Be prepared for anything that might happen because it probably will!

Dr. June Johnson

Summary:

Gather as much information about your audience as possible.

Prepare your presentation thoroughly.

Practice your delivery.

Use audio and video tapes.

Acquaint yourself with the facility and equipment.

Stay focused on the audience.

Enjoy yourself!

Chapter Ten

HANDLING FEAR

The mind is a wonderful thing. It starts working the minute you're born and never stops until you get up in public to speak.

Roscoe Drummond

Dr. June Johnson

I f you were asked to list the three things in life you fear the most, I dare say that the fear of speaking in public would be near the top of the list. According to surveys, the fear of speaking in public is stronger than the fear of dying, followed by fear of financial ruin, spiders and snakes!

Identifying fear

Fear is a normal emotion we all experience at times. It alerts us to danger. Without fear, we would probably not survive.

On the other hand, irrational fear can be a destructive, self-defeating emotion that prevents us from achieving our fullest potential. The fear that we will not measure up to our own expectations can be overwhelming. It leaves us feeling helpless and out of control.

I remember well the symptoms of fear I felt when I began performing in public - shaking knees, rapid heart beat, tight, dry throat, butterflies in my stomach, shortness of breath and an awful trembling voice.

When I was in high school, I was frequently chosen to be soloist with the choir. We had an excellent choir, thanks to a very talented and demanding musical director. We rehearsed diligently and still, by concert time, I would be a basket case.

Like a typical teen, I was far from subtle about it. After one of my mini-dramas, the director, apparently at the end of his patience, took me aside, laid his hand on my shoulder and told me how annoying I was. He told me I was being conceited. Conceited? Me? I was floored. How can you be conceited when you are so nervous that your voice and knees are shaking?

The director said I was giving no thought to the music, the pleasure it would bring to those who had come to enjoy the concert or the choir that was providing the support for my solo. I was thinking only of myself.

I'm not sure how the performance went that evening, but the director's words must have had an impact on me because I have never forgotten them. He gave me a bit of wisdom I have carried with me throughout my career as a performer.

Facing your fear

Lack of confidence, insufficient knowledge of the subject matter, lack of preparation, the fear of making mistakes or looking foolish usually cause the fear of speaking in public. Sufficient preparation and ample practice can help you control this.

When fear takes over, tension in your chest forces you to resort to costal breathing, making diaphragmatic breathing nearly impossible. Fear can force the voice into the throat, producing a tight, high-pitched, quavering sound. When uncontrolled fear is obvious to your audience, your message is compromised.

Dr. June Johnson

Controlling fear

To control fear you must first identify its cause. If you fear making a mistake or forgetting, don't take yourself so seriously. It's how you handle the situation that matters. When you make an obvious mistake, treat it casually and with humor and the audience will identify with you.

We all fear making mistakes. This is very human. But often the audience is not even aware that a mistake has been made. If the mistake is not obvious, ignore it and move on.

Determine to control your fear rather than allowing it to control you. Create as many opportunities for speaking in public as possible. Join Toastmasters, a community theater group or take a class in public speaking or dramatics. Read aloud to get used to the sound of your voice. Always practice your speech out loud.

Irrational fear can be conquered if it is faced squarely. Following are a few steps that will help you:

Identify the cause of your fear and anxiety.

Practice out loud.

Practice positive self-talk.

Recognize that making a mistake is not fatal.

Concentrate on the message.

Nerves

Although fear can make you nervous, nerves need not make you fearful. The dictionary describes nerves as "the source from which feeling, energy, or dynamic action emanates."

There is no doubt that fear and nerves are intertwined. But while fear is difficult to channel, nerves can be channeled into energy and become a positive force. When used constructively, nerves bring vitality and enthusiasm into your speech. There is more cause for concern if you do not experience some nerves before a performance. Musicians, actors, speakers, performers in all areas, rely on nervous energy to stimulate them to give a better performance. Use your nervousness to your advantage to energize, challenge and stimulate you to give a better presentation.

Summary:

Recognize your fear for what it is.

Prepare your material thoroughly.

Remember to focus on your audience.

Let your nerves energize your delivery.

Chapter Eleven

THE TELEPHONE VOICE

How you hear yourself is not necessarily how others hear you.

I n today's world, the telephone plays a critical role in business. It is an indispensable tool. The way you handle your business calls can make or break a sale or your company's image. Treat the phone as seriously as you would a personal contact. It does not matter if you are making a call or receiving one, effective telephone techniques are critically important.

Use the phone effectively

First impressions are lasting impressions, even on the telephone. They establish the mood and atmosphere of the conversation.

Following are ten tips to help you on the phone:

1. Answer the phone promptly. The suggested rule is to answer after the second ring. This enables you to prepare yourself for the call and also gives the caller a moment to prepare.

2. Prepare your greeting. Identify yourself. Keep a smile in your voice to make it sound pleasant and upbeat.

3. Speak clearly and naturally at a moderate pace. Most people speak too fast on the telephone. Without body language, the voice must do all the work.

4. Place a tape recorder by your phone and tape yourself in a conversation. You will learn how you sound to other people. Determine the changes you need to make and put them into practice.

5. Treat every caller like your best customer whether they are or not. Be courteous.

6. If you must put a person on hold, ask their permission and wait for their answer. If they agree, do not allow it to go longer than 20 to 25 seconds. A better technique might be to take their number and say you will call them back later.

7. Use your body as you speak. When you involve your body, you energize your voice. Stand up and move around or use hand gestures. Use a headset to free your hands.

8. Talk and act as though the person were standing in front of you.

9. Place a mirror before you to check your expression as you speak. If it is a pleasant one, your voice will be pleasant. If it is an unpleasant one, it will reflect in your voice and make you sound cold and indifferent.

10. Give the caller your full attention. Avoid letting distractions bother you.

Summary:

Think of the phone as an ear and use it as though it were one.

Speak to the person as though he/she were in your presence.

Smile   Smile   Smile

Chapter Twelve

LISTENING

There is only one rule for being a good talker. Learn to listen!

Christopher Morley

S o far, all of our concentration has been directed to how you can develop the power in your voice. But how you speak is only part of the equation.

Communication is a two-way street involving not only the transmitting of ideas and information but also the receiving and processing of that information. Listening is as vital to communication as speaking. It is one half of the link through which we create understanding.

When you speak, others learn. When you listen, you learn. It is important to maintain a balance between the two.

The problem

Although we are thinking creatures, most of us are very poor listeners. With so much information competing for our attention, it takes a conscious effort to maintain the attention required to listen intelligently. In today's hectic world with its constant interruptions and distractions, the average attention span is only about ten minutes. We have all become so accustomed to hearing brief messages that we are impatient and lose interest when someone takes too long to get to the point.

Active listening

Simply hearing words is not enough. You need to develop a habit of active listening.

Dr. June Johnson

Active listening is the process by which we gain the real meaning from what is being said. It requires attention and thought. Simply hearing the words is not enough, you need to focus your ears, eyes, body and brain on the speaker and process all the information coming to you through each source. What do you see? What do you hear? What do you feel? What do you think?

Active listening is like any other skill, it requires self-discipline and constant practice. Although there are courses available in public speaking, vocal skills, speech and drama, there are none I know of that train you to listen. You must make a consistent personal effort to listen intelligently.

Learn to listen

Active listening can be one of your most powerful communication tools. There is a definite correlation between the ability to listen and the ability to persuade. It is not possible to be persuasive if you have not listened carefully. This is particularly important in sales.

Fortunately, active listening is a skill you **can** master. Use body language to establish rapport with the speaker. Remain alert and maintain eye contact. Use facial expressions and simple gestures such as nodding, raising eyebrows and leaning forward to convey interest. Interject with occasional comments such as "I see" and "I understand." Ask questions to clarify a point or provide you with additional information.

Make it a point to:

>Focus on the speaker, not on what **you** are saying.

>Ignore Distractions.

>Avoid interrupting.

>Practice memory association to improve recall.

>Mentally summarize and recap the main points.

>Avoid interjecting your thoughts or anticipating the next words.

>Use body language to encourage.

>Allow time to process what you heard.

>Think before you speak.

The key to successful communication in business and social situations lies in the fine art of active listening. Pay attention and you may be surprised what you will learn.

Summary:

>Use active listening.

>Focus and paraphrase.

>Ask questions.

>Use body language.

Chapter Thirteen

CARE OF THE VOICE

Take care of your voice.
You will never have another.

D espite tremendous strides in medicine for replacing parts of the human body, it is unlikely the vocal cords will ever be replaced.

Some time ago a gentleman approached me for help. Recent surgery had left him with only one functioning vocal cord and an unpleasant, grating voice. He hoped that I might be able to help him. I was sorry to disappoint him but, unfortunately, with only one vocal cord there was very little that could be done to improve his sound.

It is important that you take care of your voice. It is the only one you will ever have.

If you find your voice is hoarse or husky, or that it becomes sore after speaking for a while, you are using it incorrectly. Bill Clinton suffers from persistent hoarseness because he is speaking from his throat. If you do the exercises in the chapter on resonance, you will help protect your voice and overcome any vocal fatigue you may experience.

The following steps will help you maintain vocal health and enjoy your voice.

> Get plenty of rest. Fatigue saps the voice of its strength and lowers the pitch.

> Drink plenty of clear fluids at room temperature.

> When speaking, always have room temperature water available.

Dr. June Johnson

Yawn to stretch and relax the throat muscles.
Use Ocean, a spray for a dry throat.

When the throat is dry or feels like cotton,
thinking of a lemon will activate your saliva
glands.

For the dry throat, Toastmasters recommends
spreading a small amount of vaseline on your
teeth to keep the lips from sticking to your teeth.

When the throat is sore, gargle warm salt water
and yawn frequently.

Avoid all milk products and sweets before a
presentation.

Breathe deeply to eliminate tension that pushes
the voice into the throat

Never force the voice to achieve volume. Rely on
your own support.

Avoid clearing the throat. It is harmful to the
vocal folds.

If you have a "frog" in your throat, simply talk
through it. Clearing does not work and can harm
the vocal cords.

Chapter Fourteen

PUTTING IT ALL TOGETHER

Success has always been easy to measure. It is the distance between one's origins and one's final achievement.

Michael Korda

W riting a book is like building a house. While it's going on, it feels like a never-ending process of decisions, challenges and delays. And yet, when it finally starts coming together, you feel great satisfaction.

That's how I feel right now. I have wanted to write this book since I founded my company, VOICE POWER, and started receiving requests from clients. They wanted written information they could use to supplement our sessions. I wrote many hand-outs and articles, but needed to collect my thoughts into a book. Now, it's done.

Or is it? Is this book an end, or a beginning?

I think it's a beginning. The house is up, the carpet's on the floor, but you have to move in. You have to paint the walls and put in the garden. You have to use your mind and muscles to make this house your own.

In this book you have information, exercises and encouragement. You can read it and put it away, or you can do the work and develop a powerful voice that is all your own.

Your job now is to practice. Make a commitment to your voice. Go back through the chapters again and again. Fit the exercises into your days. Tape yourself. Listen to the tapes. Listen to others. Notice how they listen to you. Watch your confidence grow.

Effective speech is a learned skill. But it is more than technique and beautiful tones. It is the vitality and energy you bring to your words. Whether it's one-on-one, in a meeting, on the telephone or speaking in public, if you speak from the heart, with enthusiasm and sincerity and add a smile to your eyes you will hold the attention of all who listen to you.

I wish you well. God bless and be good to yourself.

Programs

Speak with the Voice of Authority
How to develop a voice that commands and holds attention

Building Confidence and Self-Esteem
A practical, hard-hitting, no-nonsense program that will improve your self-confidence and enhance your self-image

Successful Telecommunications
Learn the secrets of a successful phone technique to achieve customer satisfaction

Does Your Voice Help Your Sales?
How to improve the bottom line with a voice that persuades

Handling the Fear of Speaking in Public
Develop techniques for facing your fear and turning it into positive energy

Audio Tapes

The Power of Your Voice
Two cassette album (2 hours) *$35*

For more information, contact:
June Johnson on Voice Power
500 West Bender Road, Suite 67
Milwaukee, WI 53217
800.988.0644
fax: 414.332.6462
VoicePwr1@aol.com
http://www.wisonline.com/VoicePower